THE AMAZING LIFE OF BUD & PAULETTE PAGE

STORIES OF
GOD'S BLESSINGS

BUD PAGE

Olympus Story House
www.olympusstoryhouse.com

CONTENTS

DEDICATION

To my wife, Paulette, who has stood faithfully by my side through good times and bad.

Then I can't forget all the wonderful people we met over the years who helped us in so many ways. Without them, there would be no story to tell.

INTRODUCTION

They say everyone has a story, and, of course, some are more interesting than others. I hope you will find our story to be one of the more interesting ones. My intention was to make these stories entertaining as well as inspirational.

As the title suggests, this is a collection of stories of how God blessed us in ways that seem almost "supernatural." I don't know any other way to explain it. When I look back over those years of my life, I see God's hand at work, and I am just as amazed as you probably will be as you read about them. All I can say is it was God who chose to bless us with success. It was all in His plan, and I choose to give Him all the glory.

I have also included a few stories that you may not consider God's blessing. You might wonder how I can include times of adversity in a book titled "Stories of God's Blessings." It's because God has taught me much in our times of adversity.

Over the years of trials and blessings, I've learned that God is faithful, and we can depend on Him no matter what. He is in control of all His creation, and He can be trusted. I pray that you will be encouraged to trust God more fully in your own life as you read about the unusual ways God chose to bless us.

CHAPTER 1

The Early Days

First, I would like to state that I am not a writer. I have just been told many times that I should write these stories down before they are lost and forgotten. These are stories of God's blessings, which have given me a life that I could never have imagined. But before I get into the good stuff, let me give you a little background.

I was born in 1945. My dad was a preacher, and my mother was a teacher. We lived very modestly and moved around a lot. We seemed to always have a little bit of land, which allowed us to have many different types of animals. My dad tried raising pheasants, rabbits, hogs, fishing worms, nutria, and even mushrooms in an effort to supplement his income. As far as I know, he never was successful at any of these endeavors. I don't know why these ventures didn't seem to work for him. As hard as he tried, we never had much when I was growing up, but I did get a pony for my birthday when I was about ten.

I guess that was the start of my lifelong love of animals, especially horses. As far back as I can remember, I wanted to be a stock farmer—you know, raising cows and horses. I really didn't think it would be possible because to raise cows and horses, you have to have land, which costs a lot of money, and I didn't think I would ever be able to afford it.

I never lost sight of that dream. In 1968, I was married and had two kids. We lived in a small house in a subdivision in the Indianapolis area, and I was in the insurance business. The house was really too small for our family, so I found one and a half acres of land and built a larger house on it. Now I had room for a couple of horses, so I bought two registered part Arabians and began taking them to shows.

One horse I bought was a three-quarter Arabian mare. Her name was Betsy, but we called her Babe. She turned out to be the best horse I ever owned. This was a bit surprising since the reason the man sold her to me was because he couldn't get near her. He told me he got her in a stall, and she kicked the side of the barn out just to get away from him. I don't know what her problem was with him, but I'm sure glad he sold her to me. I took her home and worked with her for a few days, and she couldn't have been better. The following weekend, I took her to a show, and she won first place in her class. I showed her many times, and I don't remember ever coming home without a trophy or ribbon. I broke her to ride, and she never bucked once. My daughter had her until she died at age twenty-two. Just to be sure you understand, it was the horse who died, not my daughter!

After a couple of years, we sold our house and bought a nice old farmhouse on five acres with a big barn and plenty of room for my horses. I continued to show my horses and did very well. I found something I was really good at, and before long, I was training and showing horses for other people.

This part of my life was going great, but things weren't going well in my marriage. My wife decided she wanted a divorce, and of course, I lost everything. I knew I hadn't been living right. We had stopped attending church and were living life without God, which never works for long.

CHAPTER 2

A New Chapter in My Life

Thankfully, this adversity brought me back to the Lord. One day, a friend of mine told me about a singles Bible study held at a missionary organization's headquarters. I began attending and met Paulette, who was the secretary to one of the vice presidents of the missionary organization called OMS. We began dating and eventually got married. I like to tell her that I rescued her from the "Old Maid Society."

When I met Paulette, I was working for a company that built homes all over the Midwest. I worked out of a model home in a subdivision, and I was one of their best salesmen. When I applied for the job, the regional manager interviewed me. I am only five feet two inches tall, so he asked me how I thought my height would affect my ability to sell homes. I looked at him and asked, "What does my height have to do with my ability to sell?" He said that was just the reaction he wanted from me, so he hired me. Three weeks later, we went to a seminar in Louisville, Kentucky. The regional manager was there and came up to me and congratulated me for selling three homes in the first three weeks. I thanked him and then said, "If I were only six inches taller, I would have sold three more." Of course, we both laughed, but I think he got the message.

Unfortunately, the company was purchased by a larger company, which sent notice to all the salesmen and managers stating they were terminated. It was just one week before our wedding, and I was unemployed. We went ahead with the wedding anyway. Paulette was still working for the missionary organization, so we managed to get by while I looked for a job. All I knew was sales, and I was pretty good at it.

I looked in the newspaper and found plenty of companies wanting salesmen. After applying to a few, I was finally hired by a water softener manufacturer to sell water softeners to people in their homes. The way it worked was the company would give me one appointment a day. I would go to a home where the people were getting $50 for watching my demonstration, and their friends who had previously bought from the company also received $50 for giving us their name. The company had sold me on the benefits of soft water, and if I believe in something, I can sell it. I made a sale on every one of the first seven appointments and was told this was a company record. I made $200 for each softener I sold.

Then something happened. Paulette and I went to the county fair and saw a booth where they were selling water softeners for $250. It was just like the softener I was selling for $850. After that, I tried to keep working for the company selling softeners for $850, but I just couldn't do it knowing that my customers could buy the same thing for much less if they only knew. So I quit. The boss begged me to stay and even offered to pay me a higher commission. I told him why I was quitting, but he just didn't understand that it wasn't about the money.

I then went to work for the company I saw at the fair, but they only gave me $50 per sale, and I had to find most of my own customers. I must have done well because they eventually promoted me to sales manager. This was a really hard way to start our marriage, but I knew God would take care of us if we would just trust Him. Paulette was very understanding. I think she knew I wasn't happy with what I was doing. She has truly been one of God's many blessings in my life.

We started our life together living in a mobile home park. After about a year, I thought I wanted to go to Bible College, so we moved to Fort Wayne, Indiana, where I attended Fort Wayne Bible College. Paulette was very supportive. She got a good job as the secretary to an executive of a big company. I had many odd jobs while attending college. After a year of school, I decided I should quit college and get a better job. I ended up working for a company as a wholesale carpet representative. I covered Northern Indiana and Northwestern Ohio, selling to carpet stores and builders. Things went well, and soon, we were able to buy a lot in a subdivision and move a modular home on it. We were active in a Baptist church where I led singing, Paulette played the organ, and we both taught Sunday school. After four years of marriage, our son, Lee, was born. Things seemed to be going well.

The lot we bought to put our modular home on backed up to a small piece of land that was landlocked, which means there was no access to it except through our property. One day, the man who owned the land contacted us and asked if we would be interested in buying the property. Because the price was very reasonable and he was willing to finance the land, we bought it.

CHAPTER 3

The Beginning of the Animal Business

I was used to having a little land and animals like goats and horses, so we built a barn and bought some milk goats. I like goat milk, but we were milking three goats and had more milk than we could use, so I got the idea to go to a cattle auction and buy some baby Holstein calves and raise them on goat milk. I went to an auction and bought twelve three-day-old calves, and we bottle fed them for three months. When they were ready to be weaned, I put an ad in the paper, "Three-month-old calves for sale." The phone began to ring, and before long, the calves were all sold at a good profit. To my surprise, the phone kept ringing, and people would ask about the calves for sale. When I told them they were all sold, they were so disappointed. Some even asked me to take their number and call them if I ever had more calves for sale.

This gave me an idea: why not go to the auction, buy weaned calves, advertise them for sale, and call the people who had given me their numbers? This worked really well. I even had a man call me who wanted six bred cows with calves still on them. I took his number and told him I would call him if I could come up with something. The next Monday night, I went to the auction and asked around to see if I could find someone who might have what my customer was looking for. One man told me, "That man on the front row will probably have what you want." I went down and told him my story, and he had the six cows I needed for my customer. I went home, called the man, and told him I had found his cows. We made arrangements to go see them the next day. He bought the cows and calves, and I made $350 for just finding them for him. I was having a lot of fun and making extra money we could use.

I began going to different auctions in different towns. I noticed that calves at one auction sold for less than at another auction just forty miles away. I started going to the auction that started at 3:00 p.m. I would buy a load of calves and then take them to the other auction, which didn't start until 7:00 p.m. the same day. They would sell there, and I would make $200 or more for my trouble. Now, keep in mind, this was in 1979 and 1980 when $200 was a lot more than it is today. I didn't know it then, but this was the beginning of an animal business that would last over thirty-two years.

This mobile home is where Paulette and I lived when we first got married on March 29, 1975.

Here is the modular home in Ft. Wayne.

This is the barn we built on the property we bought behind our modular home.

Our son Lee milking one of our goats at age 2 1/2.

These are Holstein calves like the ones we raised on goat milk then sold weaned at about 3 months.

This is Babe and my daughter Jodie. We had Babe until she died at age 22.

CHAPTER 4

My New Business

In 1981, the economy was really bad. The unemployment rate in Fort Wayne, Indiana, was 22 percent due in part to the shutdown of International Harvester, where ten thousand people had been employed. I was a wholesale carpet salesman, but with unemployment so high, no one was buying carpet. Builders were leaving homes half-built and shutting down subdivisions. Store owners were boarding up and walking away. People were leaving town in droves.

I needed to find something to do to support my family. It was a really tough time for us, but one day, I was at the barber shop and saw an ad in ENTREPRENEUR magazine. A company was advertising a kit for doing vinyl repair. They said you could make $20 or $30 an hour fixing rips in car seats. I thought this would be really nice if it worked, but I figured all they cared about was selling me their kit for $800. For the next few days, I couldn't quit thinking about it, so I decided to look for someone who was actually doing vinyl repair and not trying to sell me anything. I looked in the yellow pages and found a man who had just finished his third year in the business. He told me he made $80,000 in the last year. Well, that was a lot of money in 1981, and I thought if he could do it, so could I. I rode with him for about three hours the next day just to see how it worked.

I saw that to be good at this business, one had to have some natural artistic ability, especially when it comes to matching colors. God had given me the gift of color. I don't know how to explain it, but when I look at a color, I can see the colors it takes to make it. I found this out when I was in high school art class. I also have the ability to draw or paint. However, I never had the temperament for it because I could never sit in a room for hours drawing or painting. But I thought I could do this vinyl business and use all the artistic ability God had given me.

I went home and ordered the kit. When it came in, I went to a wrecking yard, got an old vinyl car seat, cut some rips in it, and started practicing. I read the manual sent with the kit and soon learned that most of what they were teaching wouldn't work if you needed to make a living doing it. I threw the manual away and began to experiment. I didn't see it then, but now, as I look back, I feel God led me to something He had given me the ability to do well. Plus, it was something I would enjoy, and most of all, I could support my family.

It was the winter of 1981, and I wanted to start my vinyl repair business. I told my wife that I didn't want to start a business where I would have to work out in the cold. I asked her what she thought about moving to Texas. She said if that is what I thought we should do, then it would be fine with her.

My sister and brother-in-law lived in Tyler, Texas. We had visited them a couple of times at Christmas, and the weather was great. My brother-in-law liked to golf, so we went golfing in December in short-sleeve shirts. This was a whole lot better than the below-zero weather we were having back in Indiana, so we decided to move to Tyler to start the business.

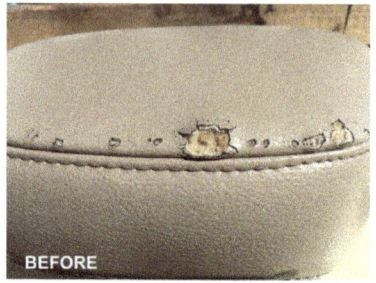 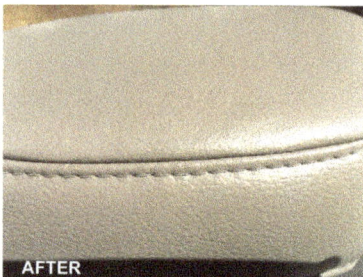

People ask me what I do. It's hard to explain so I show them these pictures I have on my phone. I've been doing this for 37 years and I still enjoy it.

I'm 73 years old and I don't know how much longer I'll be doing this, but I'm so thankful for the years I've had. They say if you can find something you like doing and you can make a living doing it you never work a day in your life.

I'm not perfect but I care about my work and that's hard to find these days.

CHAPTER 5

The Move to Texas

I moved to Tyler on March 31, 1982. I walked into car dealers and told them I had just moved here and I do vinyl repair. Most dealers were very receptive. When they asked me if I could fix something, I told them I would do my best and, if they didn't like it, they didn't owe me anything. I never had a job I didn't get paid for. At the end of the first week, I made over $300 in a town I had never lived in doing a business I had never done before. I could hardly believe how friendly the people were. I found a house to rent, and Paulette and Lee came to Tyler about a month after I did. Paulette started working through a temporary agency and soon got a permanent job as secretary to the owner of an oil company.

The house we rented was on about an acre of land. Since it was fenced and located out of city limits, I went to the local cattle auction and bought two weaned calves. The calves did well, and after a few months, I sold them for a nice profit. After renting for six months, I thought it was time to look for land to buy. I found two and a half acres on the west side of town. The owner said he would finance the land, so I bought it.

Now, all we had to do was build a house on the property. I went to the bank and told them I wanted to build a house and needed a loan. After telling them I had only been in business for six months, they said I would have to be in business for at least two years before I could get a loan. This was really discouraging to me. I bought my first house when I was nineteen, and to me, renting was just money down the drain.

I didn't give up, though. I went to all the dealers who were doing business with me and asked them to write a letter to the bank stating they were using my service, were happy with my work, and planned to continue doing business with me. It worked! I took a stack of letters to the bank, and they gave me the loan. We started building, and after living in Tyler for just under a year, we moved into our new home on two and a half acres.

CHAPTER 6

First Venture at Our New Home

Shortly after moving into our new home, I happened to be watching the program 20/20 on TV. They were doing a story on miniature horses, which were just beginning to be popular. I told Paulette that I would like to get started raising them. She didn't think that was a good idea since we really didn't have the money to get started, but I began to research them. I found two farms within driving distance, and we visited them. They both had bred mares for $3,000 each. Of course, we didn't have $6,000 to spend on miniature horses, but I couldn't quit thinking about them.

We didn't have much when we moved to Tyler. We found someone in Fort Wayne who was willing to take over our house and land for just what we owed on them. We had two old cars, but at least they were paid for, and we still had good credit. I thought maybe a bank would loan me $6,000 if I gave them my car titles. However, I went to the bank, and they said no.

Then I remembered about a company called Production Credit that made agricultural loans. I took my car titles and went to see them. I told them what I wanted to do, and they listened. After a couple of days, they approved the loan. We bought the two mares, and we were officially in the miniature horse business. To me, it was the beginning of another business, not a hobby.

I don't remember if those mares ever had babies, but I will tell you some stories I do remember. I have always had an eye for good-quality animals. If you remember, in the late 60s and early 70s, I trained and showed Arabian horses for myself and others. With that experience, I set out to buy a miniature horse I could show. I found a three-month-old filly that I bought for $2,500. We named her WC's Tinker Toy. I took her to shows and won many trophies and ribbons. Eleven months later, I sold her for $12,500. I bought another pregnant mare named Peanut. She had a little boy. At four months old, I took him to a show and sold him that day for $4,000. The miniature horse business was new, and a lot of people who knew nothing about animals were wanting to get started raising them.

I was getting a good reputation at the shows, so people began asking me to help them get started in miniature horses. I remember one year, the National Miniature Horse Show was held at the Dallas State Fair. I had nothing to show at the time, but I went to show some horses for other people. A man asked me if I could find him a mare that would win in the 32- to 34-inch class. I told him I might be able to and I would get back to him if I came up with something.

A couple of stalls over was a nice mare that had already won a championship. I found the owner and asked him if he would be willing to sell her. He said if he could get $10,000, he would sell. I told him I had a man who would buy her at that price, and I wanted a 10 percent commission. He agreed. I brought the buyer to him, and I made $1,000. That was a four-day show, and before it was over, I had sold $36,000 in miniature horses.

If you do the math, that was $3,600 I made in four days, and I didn't even have a horse at the show. Two weeks later, I was at the Louisiana State Fair and sold another $16,000 in horses for another $1,600 commission. These are just a couple of instances I remember.

CHAPTER 7

The Ups and Downs of the Miniature Horse Business

As for raising miniature horses, it's not easy. I had twelve mares one year, and I only got two babies, but I was good at buying and selling. One more example is a horse I named Midnight Magic. I bought him from a lady in Longview, Texas. He was a beautiful little 33½-inch horse. He was coal black with a white streak in his tail. I decided to break him to pull a cart. He took to it fast and moved like the wind. Only three weeks after I bought him, I took him to a show in Fort Worth. He was a high-stepping horse, what they call a park horse. In the class he was in, there was a horse named Moonlight Bay, who was the current national champion park horse, and no one had been able to beat him for three years. I didn't know what to expect since this was Magic's first show. But, when they called out the ribbon winners, Magic got second place, and Moonlight Bay got first.

The owners of Moonlight Bay tried to buy Magic from me, but I wouldn't sell. Two weeks later, at the Louisiana State Fair, we showed against each other again, and Magic beat the national champion. We were to show again the next day, but when I got to my stall that morning, some people told me Moonlight Bay's owner got Magic out of his stall in the middle of the night and measured him. Soon, the officials at the show came and told me Magic was disqualified because he was over 34 inches, which is the maximum height for a miniature horse. I couldn't believe what I was hearing. I knew Magic was only 33½ inches tall. Since they wouldn't let me show, I had no choice but to take him home.

The next day, I called the Miniature Horse Association and explained what had happened. They already knew. I told them that I wanted to take Magic to the Miniature Horse Nationals coming up in two weeks in Houston, and if they measured him over 34 inches, I would tear up his papers, take him home, and never show him again. They thought that was fair, so they allowed me to take him to Houston.

At Houston, Magic measured 33½ inches tall. I showed him in the park horse class, and Moonlight Bay was there. This was the national show, and there were lots of horses from out of state. Moonlight didn't win, and neither did Magic. I got second to a nice horse from North Carolina. When we came out of the ring, many people came up to me and said I should have won. But I did win! Magic was measured under 34 inches, and I beat Moonlight Bay again. I sold Magic that day to a farm in California for ten times what I paid for him.

This is the first house we built in Tyler.

The start of our Miniature Horse business.

This is Tinker, the one I bought at 3 months for $2,500 then sold her for $12,500 at 11 months.

This is Lee and Tinker with kindergarten class "show and tell".

Midnight Magic is the horse that beat the National Champion park horse at the Houston National Miniature Horse Show then sold for 10 times what I paid for him.

Lee having fun driving Skywalker.

After all the dirty dealing over Magic's height and some other things, I decided it was time to get out of the miniature horse business. I came home from the Nationals and made one phone call to a man in Lufkin, Texas. He came and bought all twelve of my horses, my cart, harness, horse walker, trailer, and everything else that had to do with miniature horses.

We were in miniature horses for six years. The last couple of years, we made $35,000 a year after expenses, which was a lot of money back in the eighties. I still miss the horses, but to be successful in miniature horses, you had to be at the shows. We were at shows at least three weekends a month, which kept us from attending church regularly. I knew that wasn't giving God the right priority in my life. It was really hard to give up something I was so good at, but I know I made the right decision.

Here are a couple more stories I want to tell you. I was talking to some friends and told them I was writing these stories of how God blessed us in our animal business. I told them some of the good stories, and then I told them about a little stud horse I bought from a lady in Dallas for $1,500. I knew he was really good, but he was 33½ inches tall and only a two-year-old. I thought he would probably grow to over 34 inches, so I decided to sell him. I called a man who trained and showed miniature horses for a living and told him I had a horse that would win at the shows. I felt he could even beat the current national champion. I told him what I wanted for the horse, but he said he would only give me $2,000 because the horse was probably going to go over 34 inches. This wasn't much profit, but I agreed to sell.

Two weeks later, the new owner took this horse to a show and won. He took him to several more shows and won. In just a few weeks after buying him, he sold the horse for $10,000, and that's not the worst part. In a few years, many of the horse's offspring won national championships, after which his owners sold him at auction for $156,000.

Then I told them about another horse I bought—a 27-inch stud horse named Black Diamond. I bought him as a yearling for $25,000. I took him to a show in Ft. Worth, and a man offered me $75,000 for him. I didn't sell because I had just bought him and wanted him for breeding when he was old enough. I continued to show him and did well, but when his permanent teeth came in, it threw his bite off, and I couldn't show him anymore. I eventually sold him for $8,750.

Tinker won many trophies. Here she is in Houston where she won first place.

This is Black Diamond the one I turned down $75,000 for then sold him for $8,750.

This is Skywalker and me in a pleasure driving class at the Louisiana State Fair. He always got a ribbon.

This is the little boy I sold at a show for $4,000 when he was only 3 months old. His mom's name is Peanut. She was about 28 or 29 inches.

This is the man who sold me this pig for $2,000 then bought it back for $5,000 just two months later.

My Father-in-Law with the $5,000 pig.

CHAPTER 8

The Publishing Business

Along with the miniature horses, we bought a "FOR SALE BY OWNER" magazine business. It had been in operation for about a year, and we heard the owner wanted to sell. We contacted them and made an appointment to talk about the possible purchase of the magazine. After meeting with them, we thought we could do this business. Since the price seemed reasonable at $20,000, we bought the magazine.

We soon found that publishing a magazine was a lot of work. It came out every thirty days. We just got one issue done, and then we had to get to work on the next one. My wife would do all the bookwork and typesetting on the computer. I would do all the phone work getting new advertisers, as well as calling old clients and asking them to renew their ads. We had to take pictures of the homes being advertised, sell and deliver signs, and then take the typeset proofs to the printer. When the printing was complete, we had to deliver the magazine to the stores and restaurants where we had stands marked "free." It was hard and time-consuming work.

Now, keep in mind that I was still running a successful vinyl repair business and, of course, the mini horse business, so after about two years, we decided it was time to sell. I don't remember how we came up with a buyer. I think she contacted us asking if we would consider selling. Anyway, we met and agreed on a price of $35,000, which was about our annual net profit. She agreed to give us $10,000 down and $1,000 a month until the balance was paid.

To make a long story short, every month, the magazine got smaller and smaller. After the fourth month, the magazine just disappeared along with the lady who bought it. A couple of months later, we were notified that she had filed for bankruptcy.

The reason I'm including these stories is to let you know not everything has gone as well as it could have. I'm not complaining, though, as I was right about that 33½-inch stud horse being a good one, and I did make a little money on him, and the magazine was not a total loss. Oh well, as they say, "You win some, and you lose some."

This was our FOR SALE BY OWNER Magazine.

These were the signs we sold.

We lived on this farm for 20 years and what a Blessing it was.

If you look close in the shade to the right you can see Llamas.

CHAPTER 9

Adversity

So you see, along with God's blessing, we have also had times of adversity.

I read a book recently titled *The Blessing of Adversity* by Barry C. Black, Chaplin of the United States Senate. I believe I have experienced the blessing of adversity in my life. I have learned how important it is to seek the Lord every morning. He is my refuge and my strength. I don't know how I could survive without Him. He is faithful, and I can trust Him no matter what life throws at me.

This is a fallen world, and sin in the world causes many hardships. I believe God allows hardships in a Christian's life for His own purpose, and if we are faithful and trust Him, He will bring blessings even out of our adversity. This was written in 2018 and 2019 while I was recuperating from three cancer surgeries, and although we are in our sunset years, I believe God will continue to direct us in the way we should go as long as we remain faithful to Him.

I pray that if you are going through a time of testing in your life, you are being encouraged as you read these stories. That was the whole purpose of my writing. I believe you will find peace in the midst of any storm if you turn to Him.

CHAPTER 10

What's Next

I didn't go back to a miniature horse show to watch or visit old friends for six or seven years, but I heard they were having a show in Dallas, so I decided to go. To my surprise, I saw many friends I hadn't even talked to since that show years earlier in Houston.

One couple I remember came up to me and explained a problem they were having showing their horses. They said they would pay me to come to their farm and pick out the horses they should be showing. Another man asked me to come and look at a stud horse he was thinking about buying. He wanted me to tell him if he should buy him or not. I couldn't believe people still had that much confidence in my judgment as to what was a good quality horse. I'd been out of touch so long that I didn't feel I could help either one of them, so I turned down their offers.

Now that miniature horses were out of my life, what's next? When you are used to people pulling into your driveway, writing you a check for $10,000, and leaving with a couple of horses, it is hard to get used to not having that cash flow. But before I get into "the next big thing," I have another little story that is quite interesting and a bit humorous.

I sold a miniature horse to one couple in the potbelly pig business. They asked if I would take a pig and take $2,000 off the price of the horse. I agreed to take the pig, and about a month later, someone called and offered to buy the pig for $3,000. I thanked them for the offer but decided to hang on to the pig for a while. A couple of weeks later, someone else called and asked if I would sell the pig. I told them that I had just turned down $3,000. The man asked, "Would you take $4,000?" I couldn't believe what I was hearing. This was double what I had allowed off the price of the horse just two months earlier. After thinking about it, I decided to keep the pig a while longer. This was getting interesting.

One day, not long after I had turned down the $4,000, the man I got the pig from called. I told him he wouldn't believe what had happened since I got the pig. I told him I turned down $3,000, then $4,000. I was shocked when he said, "Would you take $5,000?" Wow, this was two and a half times what I had in the pig, and the man I got it from was making the offer. It sounded crazy to me, but I told him if the pig was worth that much to him just bring me the cash, and he could have the pig.

I made good money on that pig in a short amount of time, but I was still looking for something to take the place of the miniature horses. When the man came to get the pig, I asked him if he knew of something I could raise on small acreage and make a good profit. He said I should get emus. I asked, "What are emus?" He said they were two-legged birds like a small ostrich and they were selling as fast as people could raise them. So, I started researching emus.

I found out that if you buy young ones, the older they get, the more they are worth because they are closer to breeding age. I started looking for a pair of young ones. I found a man in Iowa who would sell me two pairs of three-month-old chicks for $6,600. He was willing to meet me halfway, so we met in Joplin, Missouri. I was now in the emu business.

Sixty-six hundred dollars was a lot of money, and of course, I didn't want to lose it. But, if I lost it, it wouldn't bankrupt me or change my standard of living. I decided I would just feed these birds and see what happened. After I had them for about eleven months, a man heard about them and asked if he could come over and see them. He came and offered me $16,000 for the two pairs of emus, so I decided to sell, take the profit, and look for more.

I started getting a magazine called Animal Finders Guide, where you could find monkeys, zebras, camels, tigers, and just about any other exotic animal you were looking for. I found an ad for emus and called the number listed. They had just what I wanted, so I bought four pairs of young chicks for $13,500. Now, keep in mind that I had just made almost $10,000 on my first two pairs, so I would still have money in my pocket after buying four pairs—not much risk here.

I got the birds home and planned to keep them to breeding age and maybe hatch some chicks of my own. By this time, the market was exploding, and when something is going that well, the word gets around. One day, a man knocked on my door and said he would like to talk to me about emus. I asked him to come in, and before he left, he offered to buy my four pairs of emus for $32,000. I only had them for six months and paid $13,500 for them, so I sold them.

Now, I was not risking any money in the emu business, so I started to look for more birds. I made a deal with a man in Harlingen, Texas, to buy twelve pairs of chicks for $1,000 a pair, so we met in Lampasas, Texas, to pick up the birds. I thought I would finally keep some of these birds for breeding, but I had a problem.

We were living on two and a half acres out of the city limits, but neighbors were beginning to complain about my emu operation. A board of health representative was sent out to investigate. He said we were not in violation of any laws, but he advised us to look for a place further out of town because the complaints would probably continue unless we moved.

At church the next Sunday, I mentioned to a friend that we were looking for some acreage to put our emus on. He told me about a plot of land for sale across the road from the subdivision he lived in. Monday morning, I went to look at the property. It was "For Sale by Owner," so I called and found out it was twenty acres, and they were asking $7,200 an acre. To make a long story short, I made a deal to buy half the property—"The Best Half." The other half of the property was low and swampy and didn't really have a good pasture for raising animals.

CHAPTER 11

The House Built by Emus

God had been very good to us in our animal business and my vinyl repair business. My wife had worked herself up to a very good position at a medical clinic. We started with nothing when we moved to Tyler, but for some reason, God decided to bless us, and we were able to pay cash for the land. Now, all we had to do was build pens so we could get the emus out there. We got to work, and soon, it was ready for the birds.

Next, we had to figure out how we were going to build a house on the land and sell the one we were in. I talked to another man at church who was a home builder, and he said he could have a house built in about six months. My wife and I sat down to talk about what we wanted in the house. We put our ideas together, and I began to design the house and draw the plans. The house turned out to be much larger than we really needed—about 3,600 square feet; but we decided to go ahead with it anyway, thinking it would be a good investment. I told the builder to start building.

Now, we needed to sell the house we were in. I have never listed a house with a realtor. I figured we had six months to sell, so I stuck a "For Sale by Owner" sign in the front yard, and to my surprise, the house sold in ten days. Now what? We had to get out, and our new house wouldn't be ready for five or six months.

I had an idea. The half of the land we didn't buy had a three-room house on it. It was in disrepair and not ideal, but it might work for temporary housing. I called the owner and asked if she would be willing to rent it and, if so, how much rent she wanted. She agreed to rent to us for $250 a month, which was great. We could be right there to watch over the emus and the construction of our new home.

After we moved into the little house, I thought it would be nice to get a cheap golf cart to run back and forth between the emus and our little rental house next door. I went to downtown Tyler, where I knew of a place that sold used golf carts. The man showed me a couple and then asked me what I wanted it for. I told him I wanted it to run back and forth to take care of my emus. He asked me a few questions about them, then asked if he could come to look at them and talk some more. The next day, he came out and wrote me a check for $40,000 for two pairs of emus that I had purchased for $1,000 a pair just eleven months earlier. By the way, I did buy a golf cart for $400. Not a bad trade, huh?

I would like to say at this point that I don't know why God decided to bless us with success in our animal business. I don't have any secret formula I can share with you. All I know is it says in Proverbs 16:9 that "a man plans his ways, but it is God who directs his path."

Now, if you think what you've read so far is amazing, I have only just begun.

Things were going pretty well. The house was going up, my vinyl business was doing well, and the animal business had no signs of slowing down. I sold more emus, but I decided to keep some and hatch my own chicks. We even built a special room in the new house for incubators and newborn chicks. Once we started hatching our own chicks, I began pre-selling them for $8,500 a pair. Sales were going so well we had to finance very little on the new house. I like to say it was the house the emus built.

I loved the animal business, whether it was emus, miniature horses, potbelly pigs, or three-month-old calves, but one needs to stay on top of the business and be aware of changes in the market. After two years in the new house, I could sense the emu market slowing down. If I had sold out at the peak of the market, I would have gotten $600,000 for my emus, but by the time I sold out, I got about $75,000 for those birds. It's all about timing, but I'm not complaining, as I had already made a lot of money in the emu business.

Some people think I am a risk-taker, and maybe so, but I am a cautious risk-taker. If you remember, my initial investment in emus was $6,600, and if I had lost it, so be it. That tiny risk brought in thousands and thousands of dollars over the five years we were in the business. Just look what we would have lost if we hadn't tried. I want you to know this kind of business is risky business if you don't do it right. So many people lost lots of money in the emu business. Maybe you know some of them. What surprised me is I never advertised anywhere. All the people who bought from me came to me and I told them if they could not afford to lose the money they were about to invest, they shouldn't do it.

THE HOUSE BUILT BY EMUS

Beautiful female struts her stuff.

Very handsome male. Birds like this would sell for $20,000 a pair.

These chicks are 3 weeks old. They were all sold before they were hatched for $8,500 a pair.

This is an Emu egg. They sold for as much as $2,000 each.

This is the 2 pair I bought for $6,600 then 11 months later sold for $16,000.

Look, I'm so pretty.

CHAPTER 12

Preaching Detour

The emu business didn't last nearly as long as I had hoped, but we did very well while it lasted. It gave us a lot of good memories, and I thank God every day for the way He has blessed us.

Paulette and I have always lived below our means. God blessed us also in our jobs—me in the vinyl business and Paulette in her work in administration at the medical clinic. We both believe in a Biblical work ethic, and I believe that is part of the secret to our success. That and the belief we should be a good steward of all God gives us. It's all His, you know. He just lets us manage it for a little while, and if we manage it well and honor Him, He will give us more to manage.

Have you ever thought about why we have so much as Americans? Yes, even the poorest of Americans are blessed with much compared to people in third-world countries.

Is this true because we are somehow entitled to what we have? I don't think so. I think we should wake up every morning thanking God for His mercy, His grace, and all the undeserved good things He has allowed in our lives. I don't know why God allows some nonbelievers to achieve such success and then waste it all on ungodly living, but as Christians, I believe there is a purpose for all that God gives us, and He expects us to use it responsibly.

There are many good causes that would have no way to do the good they do if God's people didn't support them. I am so thankful that Paulette and I have found a church that believes in ministry, not only in our community, our state, and our country but all around the world. I'm so glad God has been generous to us so we can be part of these ministries by giving to the church that ministers to us.

I also believe there are ministries outside the church that need the support of believers who have been blessed - that includes all of us. Sorry, I didn't mean to start preaching. I just believe very strongly that we, as believers, should not spend all God has given us in the pursuit of our own pleasure.

CHAPTER 13

The Next Big Thing

The emu business was over, so what's next? I can't tell you how many people have walked up to me and said, "What's the next big thing, Bud?" like I was some kind of guru or something. I just told them, "I wish I knew," and I meant it.

Now, I began looking for something to take the place of the emus. I really enjoyed the emus and the people I met because of them, but they came and went too quickly. What I needed now was something I could raise and sell year in and year out. Maybe I wouldn't make the kind of money I made in emus, but I wanted something steady. Something I could count on for years to come.

I met a man in Fredericksburg, Texas, when I was selling emus. He raised all kinds of exotic animals, so I asked him what he thought I might get into that would last a long time. The first thing he said was miniature donkeys. I had been in miniature horses, but that was a rat race. It was very political, and you had to be at the shows and doing well to have a good market for your horses. He told me donkeys weren't that way. He said I could sell all I could raise for $1,200 to $1,500 each, and this had been the case for more than twenty years.

He expected the market would go on for another twenty years, so I started looking for miniature donkeys. In doing so, I found that most people were selling donkeys 34 to 36 inches with 36 inches the maximum height for a registered miniature donkey. There were a lot of people with donkeys for sale that size.

I got to thinking: how could I compete with all these other breeders? I knew that people love baby animals. I've heard many times, "They are so cute it's a shame they have to grow up." So I thought, why wouldn't smaller, cuter donkeys sell better than the bigger ones everyone else had? I learned when I was in sales that if you want to compete successfully in any market, you have to have something your competition doesn't have.

I decided I would begin looking for donkeys 30 inches or under and breed them down from there. That way, I would have something my competition didn't have, and that would give people a reason to buy from me instead of them. I began to put together a little herd of donkeys under 30 inches. I was laughed at by many, but when we began to have tiny baby donkeys, they sold fast, and some even before they were born. I found I could get more money for my smaller donkeys than the other breeders got for their bigger donkeys. Who's laughing now?

This is Nic-Nac. He was the smallest donkey I raised. He was 19 inches and 13 pounds at birth. He is now living in France.

This is just another one of our babies. We weaned them at 3 months then sent them off to their new home.

My Great Nephew Josh with one of our tiny donkeys.

This is our Great Granddaughter. Donkeys are great with kids.

I called this little girl "Miss Hollywood".

This lady came and bought 3 donkeys.

CHAPTER 14

Advent of Miniature Llamas

By now, I knew the advice telling me I should get miniature donkeys was good advice, but I wanted to do more than donkeys. I knew there were people raising llamas, and I thought I might enjoy doing the same. I started doing some research into the llama business and found many llama breeders had websites. In fact, there were thousands of breeders who wanted to sell llamas to me. This made me think—if I started raising llamas, why would anyone buy from me rather than other already-established breeders?

I thought maybe what I was doing with the donkeys would work with llamas. At this time, there was no such thing as a miniature llama, so I started calling llama breeders all over the US, asking them if they had any unusually small llamas they would sell. I found a few who would sell to me, but others said they had small ones but weren't willing to sell them.

I began putting together a little herd of smaller-than-average llamas that were shipped to me from all over the country. I made a list of breeders who were also interested in raising small llamas. After talking with many of these people, I thought there might be enough interest to start a Miniature Llama Association. If we could do that, it would add credibility to what we were doing, and if we started our own miniature llama registry, it would add value to the little llamas we would eventually be selling.

I called all the breeders on the list that I put together who I thought might have an interest in starting this association and told them what I planned to do. Every year in April in Oklahoma City, there was a big llama show and sale held at a big equestrian center. It was the biggest llama event of the year, and people came from coast to coast to attend. I told everyone we were going to have a meeting and form a Miniature Llama Association and invited them to come.

It worked, and the meeting was a success. That day in April, we started The American Miniature Llama Association. We elected officers and a board of directors. We also started the miniature llama registry. In addition to our full-time jobs, my wife and I ran the whole thing right out of our home. We published a newsletter. I designed a logo that was approved by the board. We did all the registrations and even put up a website. Believe me, it was a lot of work, but our hard work began to pay off. The regular llama association began to add miniature llama classes to their shows, and as the word spread, they started to have just miniature llama shows.

This created a demand for miniature llamas. We received calls from all over the US. We had people driving from other states to buy mini llamas from us, and we shipped many more. We were selling our little llamas for more than the big llamas were bringing, but raising llamas in Texas was not easy since it was too hot. We had to install fans and misters in the barn to help keep them cool. After about seven years of fighting Mother Nature to keep our llamas alive, we decided it was enough.

I had been President of the American Miniature Llama Association for six years, and it was doing well. We contracted with the big llama registry to do our paperwork and keep the records for a fee. This took a big weight off my wife's shoulders. Now, it was time to turn the whole thing over to someone else.

The Association allowed me to appoint my successor, so I picked a lady in Minnesota to take my place. Just like that, we were out of the llama business, but not without success. We started something that had spread all over the US and were proud of what we had accomplished. By the way, in those seven years, we met many very nice people and sold thousands of dollars' worth of mini llamas.

Acobomba is a 36-inch male. He was one of the first small Llamas I was able to find.

This is the house the emus built. We raised animals here for 20 years.

This is one of the first girls I raised. She thinks she's beautiful. I do too.

Daisy and her new baby Snowflake. I found her in Oregon.

Razado at his first show in Conroe, TX. He won Grand Champion.

Showtime is a little male I bought from some people in Kokomo, IN.

CHAPTER 15

Teacups and Munchkins

About the time we sold out of llamas, my sister told me she bought a teacup poodle she found on the internet. She said this lady in Louisiana had the best ones, but they were selling for $2,500 each. When I heard that, I began to think maybe I could do the same. I looked up the lady's website, as well as the websites of other breeders. This lady from Louisiana definitely had the best pictures on the web, but I was not convinced she had the best dogs. I searched the web and found some females not as expensive as the ones in Louisiana and started my teacup poodle business.

We raised poodles for about three years and had no trouble selling them. I would put my puppies on a website called Puppyfind.com, and even though there were over a thousand other poodles for sale on that site, ours would sell in three or four days. I don't know what made people call about our puppies rather than all the others. Maybe it was the pictures. We worked hard to get good pictures, but I like to think it was God's continued blessing on our animal business.

We decided to get out of poodles because the tiny ones were what brought the most money, and they were hard to raise. We did well while we were in the business. We shipped puppies all over the US and even shipped one to a lady in Germany. Raising puppies on a big scale was something I had never done, and I would say it was a success. But raising donkeys was much easier than raising poodles or llamas, so I began to put all my efforts into raising little donkeys.

In addition to raising donkeys, I was always looking for "the next big thing." I was still getting the ANIMAL FINDERS GUIDE magazine, and one day, I saw this ad for long-bodied, short-legged cats called Munchkin cats. The picture of the cat looked kind of like a Dachshund dog, but it was a cat. The ad said they were in great demand and hard to find. I told my wife that I was going to keep my eye on these cats because the demand could increase as word got around, and the price would go up.

About a week later, I had the TV on, and suddenly, I saw a little short-legged cat walking right toward the camera. The narration was "Munchkin cats, the biggest controversy in the cat world in decades." The show was Dateline NBC. I got my wife to come in to see what it was about. Some people wanted the cat registries to recognize the Munchkin as a new breed, but others thought it was a disgrace to the cat world.

It seems someone in Louisiana found this stray cat with a long body and short legs. It was a little boy, and they decided to keep it. It grew up and mated with their normal size female cat. When she had kittens, half of the kittens were short, like dad. When friends came over and saw the cats, they asked if they could have one. This is how it all started. Registered cat breeders thought the cats were deformed and should be destroyed.

I told my wife with this kind of publicity, the price of these cats was going to go through the roof, and I was going to find me one and get started raising them before the price was too high. I called the ad in the magazine. They didn't have any Munchkins for sale but gave me some phone numbers of others to check out.

I finally found someone in Minden, Louisiana, who had a three-month-old black male they would sell for $850. On Christmas Eve, we took off for Louisiana to buy a cat. People thought I was crazy to pay $850 for a cat. We got the cat, but he was not old enough to breed, so I kept looking. Finally, I found an adult male for sale in Wisconsin. We made a deal for $1,000 plus shipping, and I picked him up at the Shreveport airport. Now, I could get started. All I needed was adult female cats. Surprisingly, it was not hard to find adult cats that people were giving away.

The biggest surprise was the phone calls I was getting asking if I had anything for sale. Some wanted to know if I would let them just come and see the cats. One lady brought a friend and drove all the way from Albuquerque, New Mexico, just to see my Munchkins.

The most unbelievable thing that happened was when a lady from Baytown, Texas, came to just look at my two Munchkins. I made it very clear to her that I had nothing for sale, but she wanted to come anyway. When she got to our place, I showed her my two Munchkins, and she asked lots of questions. I could tell she was very interested in finding a cat so she could start raising them. Then, out of the blue, she said she would give me $10,000 for my little black boy. I reminded her of what I had told her on the phone—I had nothing for sale. Now, I would gladly have sold that cat for $10,000. After all, I had bought him for $850 just a couple of months earlier, and I now had an adult male ready to breed, so he was expendable. I knew how much she wanted that cat, so I decided to just wait and see what she would do next. I had a feeling this wasn't over yet. After I refused to sell the cat and she was ready to leave, she asked me to think about selling and, if I changed my mind, to give her a call. I told her I would, and she left.

It's about four hours from our place in Tyler to Baytown. It had been about that long when the phone rang. This lady had driven home, walked straight into the house, and called me. She asked, "Have you thought any more about selling that cat?" Of course, I had. This is just what I expected would happen.

I told her, "Lady, if you want that cat, bring me a cashier's check for $12,000, and he's yours."

She said, "I'll be there in the morning." She arrived, check in hand.

I believe that was the highest-priced Munchkin ever sold. Most of them sold for $1,500 to $3,000.

I thought Munchkins would last three or four years like potbellied pigs, but in fourteen months, it was pretty much over. I had five Munchkins left, and a lady called from Kansas. I told her what I had, and if she would come down to Texas with $2,500, she could have them all. She came, and we were out of the cat business. What really blows me away is we never advertised anywhere. By word of mouth, we sold $66,000 worth of Munchkins in those fourteen months—kind of amazing, huh?

This is a Munchkin cat. Like I said - long and short like a Dachshund dog.

Here I am with the cat I paid $850 for then sold for $12,000 two months later.

This was our pet "BUNNY". We had her for 12 years. She weighed 3 lb.

Kookie was one of our breeders. She weighed 4 lb.

Here is one of Kookie's puppies. We would sell these for $1,500 to $2,500.

This little boy was sent to Germany.

CHAPTER 16

Back to the Donkeys

Now, back to the donkeys. After a few years in donkeys, I thought I should get with the times and start a donkey website. I designed a simple site that was easy to navigate. We never had trouble selling our little donkeys, but after we launched the website, we got calls from all over—even from other countries. We had orders for donkeys that weren't even born. When we would have a new baby, I would take a picture of it when it was still wet and wobbly, email it to a waiting customer, and it was sold. This went on for years.

Over the years, we managed to breed the donkeys down to 26½ to 28½ inches tall. I sold a little 26½-inch jack to a lady in France. She bought three or four donkeys over the phone and then decided to fly to Texas and see what I had. All in all, we shipped her about fifteen donkeys, and she is now the largest breeder of tiny donkeys in Europe.

I began to notice that what I call our local market, meaning the US, was beginning to slow down, but the overseas market kept us selling right along. In the last three years we had donkeys, I know we shipped forty-plus donkeys to countries like England, France, Belgium, the Netherlands, and others. I even got calls from South Africa and Australia but never made a sale because the restrictions were too high to enter those countries, and I didn't want to mess with it. I guess our little donkeys are now known all over the world.

We had been raising donkeys for eighteen years. I was almost seventy years old, so we thought it was time to sell out. When people called or emailed us about donkeys, I asked what they were looking for, and if I had what they wanted, I would put a price on them.

As our numbers began to dwindle, I was contacted by someone representing the King of Morocco. I know that's hard to believe, but it's true. The King's son was turning ten years old, and he wanted a donkey for his birthday. What made them choose my donkeys out of all the donkeys on the internet, I don't know. I sent them pictures of two little jacks, and they picked one. Before I could take him to quarantine, they contacted me again, saying they decided it would be good to have a little jenny to go with the jack. I sent them pictures of two little jennies. They told me they couldn't make up their mind on which one they wanted, so they would just take both.

Now people ask me. How do you get three donkeys from Tyler, Texas, to Northwest Africa? All I had to do was take them about three hours away to a USDA quarantine station in Whitesboro, Texas, where they stayed for thirty days. In the meantime, the lady there had the vet come out to get up-to-date health papers on them. She built portable stalls for them to be shipped in, booked the flights out of Houston, and then took them to the airport—all this cost the King $2,700 per donkey.

Almost all animals going to Europe are flown to Paris, where they are picked up by whomever purchased them. In the King's case, he picked them up in his private jet and flew them to his country. I guess our donkeys are royalty now! Oh, just in case you are wondering, the cost of the three donkeys was just under $10,000. When you add $2,700 each for quarantine and shipping to Paris, that's a lot of money, not to mention the cost of the jet ride to their new home, but I'm sure the King could afford it.

This is the King of Morocco and his family. He bought 3 donkeys for his son's birthday.

Here is one of the 3 donkeys I sold to the King. This is the picture I sent to him.

I believe this little boy went to England.

My donkeys with new family in the Netherlands.

These are my donkeys in quarantine waiting to be shipped overseas.

This is one of our babies. We named him Tiny Tim.

CHAPTER 17

God's Next Blessing

Well, that's about it. We sold the donkeys out quickly and decided it was time to sell the farm after living there for twenty years. We thought it would be best if we lived closer to town. For most of my life, I have been able to live where I didn't have close neighbors, and I wanted to find a place where I wouldn't have to deal with the noise of kids, radios, and loud parties. After looking for a month or so, I turned down a road I knew had houses with big lots, even small acreage. Sure enough, there was a for sale sign in front of a house I really liked. I thought they would be asking more than I wanted to spend, but it was worth checking out. I drove home and asked Paulette to look it up on the computer. When we saw the asking price, we were pleasantly surprised. It was much lower than we thought it would be but still more than we wanted to spend.

I called and made an appointment to see the house the next day. It was on the south edge of Tyler and had

1 1/2 acres with 250 feet of frontage. The neighbors had two and three acres, so it was almost like being in the country. I won't go into the details about the house but will say we both liked it. I told the real estate agent what I was willing to pay, which was a good bit less than what they were asking, and he wrote up the offer. I decided if they counter-offered, I would go up $5,000 and no more, even though the asking price was a fair price.

The next day, the homeowner countered back exactly $5,000 over our offer, so we accepted, and the house was ours. When we first looked at the house, the homeowner was there and asked us if we had a house we had to sell. I told her yes, we did, and she asked, "Then why are you looking at mine?" I told her because I don't have to sell my house to buy yours. She was very nice after that. I think it might have had something to do with her willingness to sell to us at a lower price. Before we started looking, I had made arrangements with the bank to finance the new house until we could sell the farm. Once we sold the farm, we could pay off the new house. I figured it might take six months to sell our house, and I could make the payments until then.

As I said before, I always sold by owner, but I had never sold a house at the price we were asking for the house on the farm. I decided I would put a "For Sale by Owner" sign in the front yard and give it thirty days. If it didn't sell, I would talk to someone about listing it. If it sold by owner, I would save about $24,000 in real estate commissions.

Our sign was up on Friday, and we got a few calls on the weekend from people, mostly asking what we wanted for the house. Monday night, I got a call from a realtor who told me she had a client who wanted to see our house. I told her she could show it if it didn't cost me anything. She brought a lady out the next day. She loved the house. Her husband was at work, so she called him and told him he needed to come see the house now. He managed to get off work and was there within thirty minutes. He looked around the house a bit, then walked out to the barns and looked at the land. We were standing in one of the barns when he asked me if I would take a little less than what I was asking. I told him I would, and then he said, "You can take down the sign your house is sold." Wow, it sold in four days by owner! As I always say, "You never know till you try."

By the way, the house we bought in town had to have some remodeling done, and the owner asked for three weeks to get out, so the people buying our house gave us two months before we had to move. We closed on our new place one week after our farm sold. We never had to make the first payment on our new house. We just paid it off after we closed on the farm.

CHAPTER 18

To God Be the Glory

Now, all I can do is look back at all the ways God has blessed us. These stories are stories of God's blessings. I don't know any other way to explain it. After all, how many people do you know who have sold something to the King of a foreign country? And who sells a cat for $12,000? I have told these stories many times, and I can hardly get through them without tears coming to my eyes. God has led us all the way. I am overwhelmed when I think of God's grace given to us. It has been better than I could ever have imagined.

In just over thirty-two years, we sold well over a million dollars' worth of animals. I have been told more than once that I should write a book. I asked one man what I would write about, and he said, tell how you did all this. People would like to know. I told him it would be a short book and not very interesting. I fed and took care of the animals, and God took care of the sales.

In the beginning, I told how I always wanted to be a stock farmer but didn't think I would ever have the money to get started. Well, guess what I did for over thirty-two years? I also think God gave me the ability to do my vinyl business very well, which I have been doing for thirty-seven years, and I still enjoy doing it. We are active in a great church. Yes, we have had some hard times in our lives as well, but we have had the support of our wonderful Christian friends and, of course, our family.

Paulette and I have been married for forty-four years, and we are a great team. I always tell her she was God's gift to me and, if you know us, you know who got the best end of that deal. I know none of this would have been possible without her support. We don't know what the future holds, but we know Who holds the future, and we choose to follow Him.

There you have it. No big secret. Just trust God to lead and be willing to follow. I believe God led Paulette and me to Tyler, Texas, for His own purpose. He chose to bless us beyond our wildest imagination for reasons known only to Him. How can we do anything but praise Him and give Him the glory for all the great things He has done in our lives.

It says in Psalm 37:4, "Delight yourself in the Lord and He will give you the desires of your heart." Looking back on the last thirty-seven years, I can think of nothing in the world I would rather have done.

I hope you have enjoyed these stories of God's blessings. I want you to know it is God who made these things happen. I take no credit for any of it. I was just along for the ride, and what a ride it has been. God has surely given me the desires of my heart, and I am humbled by all He has done.

To God Be The Glory!
Amen.

Here is where we live now on 1 1/2 acres. It is quiet and about as close to the country as you can get.